IMAGES
of America

CLEVELAND'S
DEPARTMENT STORES

IMAGES
of America

CLEVELAND'S
DEPARTMENT STORES

Christopher Faircloth

ARCADIA
PUBLISHING

Copyright © 2009 by Christopher Faircloth
ISBN 978-0-7385-6076-2

Published by Arcadia Publishing
Charleston, South Carolina

Printed in the United States of America

Library of Congress Control Number: 2008939660

For all general information contact Arcadia Publishing at:
Telephone 843-853-2070
Fax 843-853-0044
E-mail sales@arcadiapublishing.com
For customer service and orders:
Toll-Free 1-888-313-2665

Visit us on the Internet at www.arcadiapublishing.com

CONTENTS

ACKNOWLEDGMENTS

First and foremost I would like to acknowledge my family, Jalen, Kendell, and Kim, for being all-around great people and for putting up with me all this time. I would also like to thank my parents, who have not disowned me yet (but probably should have a long time ago). I cannot forget my brother Tim, mainly for making me look so good in comparison. I kid! Let's make millions!

I would also like to thank the people who assisted me in procuring the images in this book. Those include Lynn Duchez-Bycko and Bill Barrow of the special collections department at Cleveland State University, whose ninjalike prowess in locating original photographs was a great help. Also of note is Elmer Turner from the photograph collection at the Cleveland Public Library, whose assistance in hunting down great photographs and making department store–related eating suggestions was second to none. Thanks to John Awarski and Rob Sirn of Traditions Alive for providing pictures and for helping to keep Mr. Jingeling around for a new generation. Also thanks to Howard Tucker of Mort Tucker Photography for being gracious in allowing the use of a certain vintage Mr. Jingeling shot. And lastly for pictures, I would like to thank the Library of Congress for posting print-quality historical images online—it is good to see my tax dollars at work!

I also owe a debt of gratitude to my former work crew, whose support of this project was greatly appreciated. I hope they are all doing well in their new endeavors, whatever they may be.

To Melissa Basilone, my editor, thank you for your assistance and understanding and for giving me a great dinner party line: "I am a published author."

Several publications were helpful in putting all the pieces together for this book. Those include James M. Woods's *Halle's: Memoirs of a Family Department Store, 1891–1982*, published by Geranium Press, 1987; Richard Karberg's *Silver Grille* series of books, published by Cleveland Landmarks Press; *The Encyclopedia of Cleveland History*, edited by David D. Van Tassel and John J. Grabowski and published by Indiana University Press; *The Way We Shopped*, written and produced by Bob Becker and Luanne Bole-Becker and released by WVIZ-PBS, 2000; and William Ganson Rose's *Cleveland, The Making of A City*, currently published by Kent State University Press.

Unless otherwise noted, photographs are courtesy of Cleveland State University's Cleveland Press Collection.

INTRODUCTION

Cleveland has a long and rich history of retailing in general and department stores specifically. The trade of goods and services in the city can be traced back to the first trip to the Western Reserve made by city founder Moses Cleaveland in 1796, when he negotiated his claim to the area by exchanging goods with local Native American tribesmen. Since those early times, Cleveland has grown to become a major American city, and as the city grew, so did its retailers.

Many of the large department stores that dominated the city's retail scene in the 20th century—such as Higbee's, Halle's, and the May Company, among others—could trace their origins to small dry goods stores in the 19th century. Higbee's, for example, can be traced back to the Hower and Higbee Dry Goods Company store, which opened in 1860. Located on West Superior Street just off Public Square, the store was founded by John Hower and Edwin Higbee. Halle's originated with the purchase of the T. S. Paddock and Company hat and fur store by brothers Salmon and Samuel Halle in 1891. The store, also initially located on Superior Street, was funded with seed money from their father, Moses, himself a successful businessman. The May Company of Cleveland, a branch of the nationally known May Company of St. Louis, originated with the 1899 purchase of the E. R. Hull and Dutton Company store on Public Square—a franchise that has its own lengthy history.

As Cleveland grew and prospered, so did the department stores that supplied household goods to the growing ranks of its citizens. During the first third of the 20th century, all of Cleveland's major department stores, including Bailey's, Taylor's, and the various incarnations of Sterling-Lindner, went through explosive stages of growth. Nearly all the stores moved up to larger quarters or expanded, and in many cases they did both. Taylor's moved to larger digs on Euclid Avenue. The May Company added space, with frontage on both Ontario and Euclid Avenues, and then built upward, becoming the largest department store in Ohio. Higbee's moved up to Playhouse Square and then back down again to anchor the Van Sweringen's massive Cleveland Union Terminal project. Even Halle's built in Playhouse Square, added, and expanded, winding up with sales facilities on two separate city blocks. The competition between all the department stores and their smaller competitors was intense, but industry in Cleveland was in full swing and there were plenty of shoppers to make the rounds up and down Euclid Avenue, Cleveland's premier retail corridor.

After World War II, suburbanization gripped Greater Cleveland as it did in much of the rest of the United States. Some, such as Higbee's and The May Company, embraced the trend and spread their reach into the suburbs and, later, into outlying counties, extending their viability for most of the rest of the century. Bailey's, an early adopter of suburban branches, continued its reach outward but with less of a lasting effect. A unique approach to this new trend was taken by Sterling-Lindner, who bet everything on the viability of its Playhouse Square store and ultimately lost.

The story of Cleveland's department stores is one that follows the fortunes of the city itself. When Cleveland was booming so too were the stores, and when the city began to suffer, the department stores suffered as well. But what was perhaps most impressive was the mark on the collective consciousness of Clevelanders young and old that the stores made during their tenure here. Traditions that still continue in the 21st century, like Mr. Jingeling, originated with stores that no longer bear their names on the cityscape. Mr. Jingeling, Santa's elf that saved Christmas with his key-making skills, still entertains the children of northeast Ohio, most of who are far too young to have ever even seen a Halle's store, let alone shopped in one.

Other new traditions have come about because of Cleveland's rich retail history and environment. Once the holiday shopping season cranks up in November, few with electricity and a television can avoid the perpetually shown 1983 holiday classic *A Christmas Story*. As any Clevelander worth his salt knows, *A Christmas Story* is filled with many scenes shot in the area, from Higbee's on Public Square to a nondescript house in Tremont. Cleveland was chosen precisely for its ability, even in the early 1980s, to invoke the feeling of Christmases of the 1940s and the environment (and shopping) that existed during that time frame. For many of those familiar with Cleveland's great retail history, each time they mouth the words to the movie that they have heard so many times before, they recall their own childhoods shopping at that very Higbee's, or at Halle's, or May's, or any number of retailers that used to occupy Cleveland's opulent Euclid Avenue.

In *Cleveland's Department Stores* the images depicted are but glimpses in time, reminders of what great shopping and what great companies used to be. But more importantly, this collection of images is intended to remind the readers of their own experiences, be it riding the bus downtown to shop, getting a cardboard key from Mr. Jingeling, or enjoying a delicious meal at the Silver Grille. For those who never got to enjoy the Christmas trees at Sterling-Lindner or visit the Frosty Bar with their parents, *Cleveland's Department Stores* is still an enthralling look at what a grand and all-encompassing experience Cleveland's department stores used to provide.

One

FROM ONE ROOM TO ONE BLOCK

Starting with simple one- or two-room dry goods stores, the path of Cleveland's department stores mirrored the growth of the city itself. Although many came about during the latter half of the 1800s, each had its own unique story behind how it came to be. Halle's came about from a loan made from a successful father to two eager sons; Taylor, Kilpatrick and Company made history with its one-price, no-haggle policy; and the May Company bought its way into Cleveland by taking over E. R. Hull and Dutton in 1899. Whatever their origins, the exponential growth during the 1800s and the early part of the 20th century set the stage for the great department stores that are so fondly remembered today.

Intertwined with the history of Cleveland's department stores is the history of Cleveland's best-known thoroughfare, Euclid Avenue. During much of the 1800s, the finest establishments were located on Superior Street (now Superior Avenue), so much so that Taylor, Kilpatrick and Company created a stir when it located to the Cushing Block at the base of Euclid Avenue in 1870. Slowly Euclid Avenue became the desired location for retail establishments, and as the stores crept up the avenue, they replaced the stately mansions that had existed there for decades housing Cleveland's most notable families. Millionaire's Row, as it was called then, was pushed farther and farther eastward as grass was replaced by brick and traffic. By 1910, when both Halle's and Higbee's opened their new stores in Playhouse Square, the stage was set for the premier shopping avenue in Cleveland.

It was truly a time of unabashed growth for the city and subsequently for the retail trade located there. Be it economically or physically, in the early days of retail Cleveland's department stores helped shaped the cityscape for decades to come.

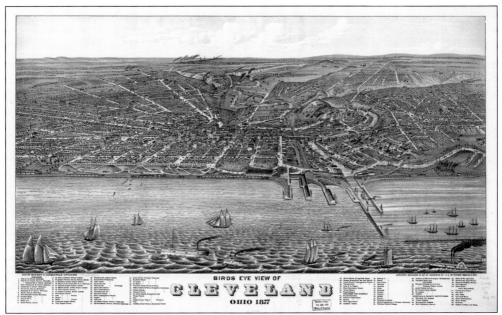

Cleveland's department stores originated in the 1800s when the city was growing by leaps and bounds but was still small compared to the metropolis it has become. (Library of Congress Map Collections.)

For many years Euclid Avenue, Cleveland's main retail thoroughfare, was lined with beautiful mansions populated by the city's elite. As retail and commercial buildings slowly ate their way up residential Euclid Avenue in the coming years, by 1910, Higbee's new store would occupy this site, with Halle's mirroring the opposite side of the street with a new store as well. (Cleveland Public Library Photograph Collection.)

Brothers Salmon and Samuel Halle founded the Halle Brothers store in 1891 by purchasing an existing hat and fur apparel shop on Superior Street. By that time, retail activity had already shifted toward Euclid Avenue, and after a successful start the brothers moved their shop to the Nottingham Building near present-day East Fourth Street (right side of photograph). (Cleveland Public Library Photograph Collection.)

When the new Halle's building was completed at what is now called Playhouse Square, it was considered to be a state-of-the-art facility. From the photograph it can be seen that at the time this area of Euclid Avenue was not built up yet. The area farther east from the store was still considered Millionaire's Row (named for all the mansions along the avenue); however, encroaching commercial and retail development (such as Halle's) was rapidly eroding the residential nature of the street.

Halle's deliverymen pause for a photograph with their horse and delivery carriage around the early 20th century.

The May Company was a new name in Cleveland when this picture was taken in 1899. Headquartered in St. Louis, the May Company made its introduction to the area by purchasing the E. R. Hull and Dutton Company on Ontario Street near Public Square and subsequently changing the name to the May Company. Shortly after this photograph was taken, a three-story addition was made to the building to complement existing sales space. "Watch Us Grow" would be a slogan that stuck with May's through many decades.

Within a few years, the May Company of Cleveland management realized it needed additional sales space as well as frontage on Euclid Avenue. It hired nationally known architecture firm Graham, Anderson, Probst, and White to design a large addition that would front Euclid Avenue, while still connecting through to its other buildings on the block. The addition, seen above, was completed in 1915 and gave the May Company an L-shaped facility that stretched from Euclid to Ontario Street.

Much of downtown was residential in nature before it was overcome by retail and commercial development. An example of this would be the Cushing mansion, which stood on the site that the May Company would later occupy. The Cushings were notable as the family line contained generations of prominent doctors, including medical pioneer Harvey Cushing, who is considered to be one of the foremost innovators in modern neurosurgery.

In April 1969, a plaque was dedicated at the May Company store recognizing the site as the birthplace of Dr. Harvey Cushing. On hand for the dedication were Mrs. Henry Cushing, Gov. Jim Rhodes, Dr. E. Harvey Cushing, and Henry Cushing.

The picture above depicts the sales floor at the May Company around the early 20th century. At this point in time, stores were full-service affairs, where clerks fetched goods from shelves to present to customers.

In the days before automobiles dominated city streets, it was common for all types of retail establishments to offer delivery service for customers. Although convenience was a factor in the popularity of home delivery, many times there was a certain prestige from having packages home delivered from a particular store. The photograph above shows an early-20th-century May Company delivery wagon parked on an as-yet-unpaved city street.

The May Company slogan, Watch Us Grow, reached out from the city and into the rural Ohio countryside. Much like the stereotypical barn tobacco advertisements, the May Company had a few of its own barn-side as well. Into the 21st century, remaining May Company barns could still be found in Portage and Ashtabula Counties.

For more than half a century the Bailey Company and the May Company were separated by just one wall. (Cleveland State University's Cleveland Union Terminal Collection.)

The Bailey Company, much like its competitors, had a long history in Cleveland. Originating in 1881 as a small dry goods store, the company gradually grew larger by acquiring competitors and adding more lines of goods. From its inception, the Bailey Company maintained its flagship location at the corner of Prospect and Ontario Avenues—once the site of an early cemetery. The picture above, dated 1949, shows its 7-story building built in 1907 (right), which was quickly added to with a 10-story addition (left), erected just three years later.

Sterling and Welch was one of a handful of predecessors to Sterling-Lindner. Beginning on Superior Street in 1845, the store originated without either Sterling or Welch. By 1889, George Welch and Frederick Sterling had taken control of the company and by 1902 had reorganized it as the Sterling and Welch Company. The store was moved to the Playhouse Square location seen at right in 1909 and was joined—at the wall—by Higbee's the following year. (Cleveland Public Library Photograph Collection.)

Enveloped in racks of clothes, Elizabeth Chisholm and Elizabeth Cross have tea at the Lindner Company store in Playhouse Square. The Lindner Company was another of the forerunners of Sterling-Lindner. Named for Max Lindner, one of the initial partners to start the business in 1908, it was initially located on East Ninth Street. In 1915, it moved to the larger store, seen above.

Taken from Public Square in 1870, this shot shows St. Paul's Church and a portion of the Cushing Block, visible on the right. In addition to being built on the future Euclid Avenue location of the May Company, the Cushing Block was also the initial home of Taylor, Kilpatrick and Company, forerunner of the Taylor Company, which opened the same year. A central theme of the store involved selling items at one price for everyone, instead of negotiating prices with each customer. (Cleveland Public Library Stanley L. McMichael Collection.)

In 1907, the store now known as William Taylor Son and Company built a new five-story building at 630 Euclid Avenue, followed by an additional four stories in 1913, bringing the building to nine stories (seen in the photograph above around 1934).

Founded in 1860 by Edwin Higbee and John Hower, Higbee's was a simple two-man dry goods store originally known as Hower and Higbee's located on Superior Street near West Third Street. By 1870, it had moved to a larger building across the street. Following Hower's death in 1897, the store incorporated as the Higbee Company. It expanded once more in 1904 and relocated in 1910 to Thirteenth Street and Euclid Avenue. This picture depicts the store's early locations through 1904.

At the heart of Playhouse Square, Higbee's faced the Halle Brothers Company. Initially the building had four floors with decorative trim at the top and bottom. Later a fifth floor was added and the matching top trim eliminated. In 1929, Higbee's was purchased by the Van Sweringen brothers, forefathers of Shaker Heights and the east side rapid transit system. In 1931, Higbee's moved to the Cleveland Union Terminal Complex on Public Square. (Cleveland Public Library Photograph Collection.)

Doorman Ernest C. Speck stands at attention outside the Higbee Company in this image dating from the early 20th century. The location depicted is the earlier Higbee building at Thirteenth Street and Euclid Avenue, prior to its move to the Cleveland Union Terminal Complex.

An early-20th-century photograph depicts a horse-drawn carriage and carriage men parked outside the front entrance of Higbee's Playhouse Square location.

Two

HEYDAY OF CLEVELAND'S DEPARTMENT STORES

The heyday of Cleveland's department stores, as many current Clevelanders would remember it, truly began with the late 1920s and early 1930s. By this time most of the stores would be settled into the locations that they would be known for for the rest of their viable days, while many great shopping traditions would gain a foothold on the collective consciousness of millions of northeast Ohioans. By the late 1920s, Halle's would already have its stores on both sides of Euclid Avenue and Sterling and Welch would have introduced the beginning of a long line of gigantic Christmas trees. In 1931, the truly amazing Higbee's store opened to much fanfare at the base of the even more amazing Cleveland Union Terminal, and, not looking to be outdone by a competitor, the May Company debuted its remodeled store across the street. Despite the major economic slowdown during the Great Depression, Cleveland's department stores soldiered on, with each of the six major department stores—Halle's, Higbee's, the May Company, Bailey's, Taylor's, and the Sterling-Lindner predecessors—all making it through the difficult time intact.

Through the 1940s and 1950s, industry—and war—roared and the stores roared right along with it. The major department stores were a focal point of activity; they served up everything from fashion shows to ice-cream dishes for a generation of Clevelanders. And although the suburbs began to loom in the distance, Euclid Avenue was still the undisputed queen of the northeast Ohio shopping scene.

In the late 1920s, Halle's maintained retail stores on both sides of Huron Road. To make it more convenient for customers to commute from separate buildings (as well as to dodge the winter cold), Halle's submitted a proposal for a pedestrian bridge to connect the two buildings. The proposal was vehemently opposed by neighboring merchants. It was also rumored that the Van Sweringens also had a hand in suppressing the footbridge. The plan was defeated and never built, although the buildings were connected via an underground tunnel.

Like many other establishments of the time, the lunch counter at Halle's was a popular spot to grab a bite to eat, even during the tumultuous depression. Seen in the background is the perennial favorite, the soda fountain. Shown in the foreground are (from left to right) waitress Leona Tinn, Dorothy Town, Arline C., Nettie Symes, and Mary Praynor Walsh.

Like many things in the 1930s, art deco was the style of choice in the Halle's fur salon.

In December 1931, the Higbee Company was in the midst of constructing a new store on Public Square. The move would return the Higbee Company back to Public Square after nearly a quarter-century stint across from Halle's on Playhouse Square. When completed, the new store stood as an anchor to the new Cleveland Union Terminal Complex, which became the hub of the city's rapid transit system. This photograph faces south from Ontario Avenue. (Cleveland State University's Cleveland Union Termina Collection.)

The Van Sweringen brothers' massive Cleveland Union Terminal project was the ultimate impetus for Higbee's returning to Public Square in 1931. As a hub for both train travel and their Shaker Rapid Transit system (seen here), the brothers wanted to capitalize on the captive traffic by incorporating a department store into the project. When the pair failed to lure Halle's (or other department stores), they solved their dilemma by simply buying Higbee's and moving it there themselves. (Library of Congress Historic American Engineering Record.)

Part of the Higbee's first-floor sales area is seen from above on opening day of the new store on September 8, 1931. Although the Cleveland Union Terminal and associated buildings (like Higbee's) were a major draw, the economic problems of the time drew more lookers than shoppers during Higbee's early days there.

The first purchase at the new Higbee's opening day on September 8, 1931, was reported to have been captured in the image above. The lucky two making their purchases at the jewelry counter are Mrs. E. G. Minard of Alliance (left of counter, front) and her daughter Mrs. L. I. Thurnhorst of Lakewood (left, behind).

Higbee's clerks are deep in contemplation while manning the counter at the new Higbee's store.

Many loyal Higbee's shoppers can still recall the clacking of the wooden steps on the Higbee's escalators. Although a mundane aspect of department store shopping today, the state-of-the-art escalators at Higbee's in 1931 warranted their own promotional photograph.

Part of the cavernous first-level sales floor at Higbee's is shown prior to the initial opening of the store on September 8, 1931.

The plush second-floor fashion salons were accented with an ample amount of woodwork. In the rear was a gown room and model display.

The living room furniture department was located on the seventh floor of the new store. Finely crafted wood furniture was complemented by plush sofas and sitting chairs. In the rear of the department was the boudoir shop.

The beauty salon was located on the sixth floor. Aside from some of the decorative flourishes that were found throughout the store, the salon was paneled with beautiful African wood and featured a crystal-inlaid ceiling.

The manicure area of the salon was put to work on opening day.

Like many department stores, Higbee's offered a bargain basement on the lower level of the store. The store sold clearance and lower-priced goods to those who either could not afford to purchase the wares on the main floors or were simply looking for a deal. Many former customers will also recall it as the location of the delicious Frosty Bar ice-cream parlor.

To compete with the new Higbee's store being built at the Cleveland Union Terminal, the May Company made renovations to its store, also on Public Square. Part of the renovations included the third-floor millinery, or women's goods, department. This photograph is a shot of the women's hats, with the corset display at the rear of the aisle.

Two months after Higbee's grand opening at the Cleveland Union Terminal, the May Company held its own grand opening for its renovated store. The exciting event brought out the president of May's national corporation, Morton J. May (far right, hat in hand), and the wife of the May Company founder, Mrs. David May (left, in front of man in hat). Rounding out the group is Nathan Dauby (left of Morton J. May), who worked in many facets of May's Cleveland branch for more than half the 20th century.

Casual observers may have a hard time identifying the outward change resulting from the May Company's 1931 renovations. Although the Public Square May's building looks almost the same as it did five years earlier, a quick count of the windows shows an additional two floors were added. The May Company store, with all its additions and renovations, continued to live up to the oft-advertised "Ohio's largest department store."

Elegant and modern for the time period, the shoe salon is depicted after the 1931 remodel.

Not to be outdone by Higbee's, Fire Chief James Grauger, W. D. Guion, and S. M. Gross examine the May Company's escalators prior to the grand reopening of the Public Square store.

A crowd surrounds a "blue" eagle caged at the front of Bailey's downtown in 1934. The blue eagle was a part of an expansive federal campaign to encourage businesses to comply with the National Industrial Recovery Act, part of Franklin D. Roosevelt's New Deal. Companies that complied with such regulations as a minimum wage, standardized workweek, and elimination of child labor were able to post the blue eagle poster or logo on their premises.

Silent movie star Colleen Moore's miniature fairy castle visited the May Company in 1935. Moore, fond of dollhouses and helping children, toured her intricate castle in department stores nationwide, raising money for children's charities. The castle's chandeliers featured real diamonds; the floors were covered with bearskin rugs; the shelves had minute, worded books; and the walls were adorned with miniature murals by Walt Disney. The castle is now on display at the Museum of Science and Industry in Chicago.

As time and technology progressed, horse-drawn delivery wagons gave way to small electric cars, and then to trucks. The impeccable Halle's truck—produced by Cleveland-based White Motors—and deliverymen are seen above delivering goods to some of the well-to-do in the then relatively new suburbs in 1930. Having boxes of the latest wares delivered by a Halle's deliveryman was a status symbol in the early 20th century.

While many industrial plants in the city rumbled with activity through the night, the hustle and bustle of Cleveland's department stores during the day gave way to stillness in the predawn hours. This 1938 photograph shows a deserted Euclid Avenue with Halle's on the left and Sterling and Welch on the right. The Hotel Statler's sign can be seen on the right in the distance, while streetcar tracks line the middle of the street.

In 1938, Higbee's featured a display sporting a mannequin in an Indians jersey reading, "This is the shirt that cost Johnny Allen $250.00." Johnny Allen, pitcher for the Indians, had recently been fined $250 for refusing to trim a red undershirt, which had a ripped sleeve that flapped as he pitched, distracting opposing batters. The shirt was procured by Indians owner Alva Bradley, who passed it along to his brother Charles, who had recently become part owner of the Higbee Company.

In 1939, the May Company debuted the first Crosley car model. Costing only $250 and averaging 50 miles per gallon on the highway, the Crosley car was affordable for most people. At that time the public favored larger cars over smaller, and the Crosley Car Company ceased production in 1952. Interestingly, Halle's looked into selling Crosleys but was thwarted by state laws preventing department stores from being car dealers. In this picture, Lee Herman takes a pretend spin at the wheel while Mary Ruth Lavoo looks on.

Customers file through the main sales floor at Halle's in December 1939. Halle's was considered to be one of the finest establishments in Cleveland to do holiday shopping.

In 1939, a majority interest in Taylor's was quietly bought by the May Company, although they continued to operate as separate entities. (Cleveland Public Library Photograph Collection.)

A popular feature of the May Company store was the children's playground, where shoppers could take their kids for a bit of fun in between perusing the latest fashions. By this time, the playground was a well-ingrained staple of Cleveland shopping, having been introduced at the store in 1904. Frills such as children's playgrounds, beauty salons, restaurants, and the like were common features of the large downtown department stores.

As part of kids' entertainment, Higbee's featured a life-size replica of a Chesapeake and Ohio locomotive cab named the Can-Do Special. The setup was complete with a functioning train whistle and bell, which delighted children but was of questionable excitement for parents. When the child engaged the throttle, a screen outside the "window" of the cab scrolled a simulated view of the landscape that would be seen when riding on a real train, making for a realistic ride for youngsters at the helm.

In the mid-1940s, it became apparent that Halle's needed to expand. With Playhouse Square being developed, it took a creative plan to provide the space that was needed for the bustling store. In April 1947, architectural firm Walker and Weeks presented the design for a seven-story addition facing Prospect Avenue. The most creative part about the addition was that a portion of it would actually be built over the East Twelfth Street alley, allowing the roadway to run through the building. Over some opposition the plan was approved and built, and the alley was rechristened Halle's Alley.

A pair of panty hose rarely brings much excitement in the 21st century; however, this 1946 shot of the Bailey Company sales floor shows exactly how thrilling discounted panty hose can be. In an image simply captioned "Rush at Bailey Co. nylon sale," these World War II–era women pack into the store with great enthusiasm for the low-cost leg wear.

A group of children closely watches the action of the miniature Ernie's Circus, which appeared at Halle's in 1952. Ernie's Circus was the creation of Ernie Palmquist (rear), who, with his wife Virginia, traveled the country displaying the intricate set. The circus, hand carved by Ernie, was made up of over 25,000 pieces, including the circus trains, animals, and performers, which were animated using 25 electric motors. Halle's hosted the display for the benefit of the Infantile Paralysis Foundation, which received the proceeds from the 10¢ per person admission fee.

A saleswoman does her best to assist a Higbee's customer in picking just the right fragrance for that special someone at home.

This view shows the Halle buildings in 1953. The white building in the top center area is the original 1910 building with a 1949 west wing addition. The white building at the bottom right is the Huron-Prospect Building with the late-1940s annex on the right-hand side. Looking closely, one can see the entrance for East Twelfth Street/Halle's Alley that runs through the building (fourth row of windows from the right, ground level).

In 1953, industry in the area was still operating at full tilt, with many factories, foundries, and plants spewing smoke and other pollutants into the air. The soot and grime that was deposited on buildings was no more evident than on Halle's as workers went about cleaning the exterior of the building. The white portion (left, center) is the cleaned, original color of the terra-cotta facade, while the gray-brown portion of the building (right) is uncleaned and still covered in filth.

This 1954 shot shows the throngs of shoppers walking west down Euclid Avenue in front of the May Company building. On the far left, a crowd is visible admiring May's holiday decorations in the display window. In the distant right stands the Cleveland Union Terminal, with Higbee's located just around the corner and to the left (not visible).

Forest Ottinger, the operations manager at Bailey's, goes over some of the day's figures with one of his employees in the men's furnishings department in September 1955.

In 1956, Halle's commissioned New York artist Daniel Rasmussen to paint a mural in the new tearoom on the ninth floor of the store. The extensive painting, measuring approximately 178 feet by 15 feet, was based on the Greek legend of the Minotaur, and as a result the room was dubbed the Minotaur Room. A *Cleveland Press* newspaper article released at the time reported that it was rumored that Rasmussen painted the mural with no advance sketches or preparation.

Throngs of shoppers cross in front of Higbee's at the intersection of Euclid and Ontario Avenues in 1958. Although expansion of retail into the suburbs had already begun by the time this photograph was taken, downtown still retained its throne as the center of Cleveland shopping.

Four-year-old Robbie Hunt of Parma does his best to coax a smile from the British guard outside Halle's in 1959. The guard was on hand to protect an English country village that had been constructed on the seventh floor of the store. While Hunt put up a valiant effort, the guard refused to crack a smile.

The Halle's facade is made up of intricately designed terra-cotta. Trivia buffs may also note that Halle's was the inspiration in the naming of actress Halle Berry, a native of nearby Bedford. Oddly enough, she once worked for rival Higbee's.

Contrary to the national chains of today where most goods are brought in via truck from regional warehouses that may be tens or hundreds of miles away, Cleveland's department stores kept their warehouses close to their stores. In the case of Sterling-Lindner-Davis, close meant right out the back door of its Euclid Avenue store. The Sterling warehouse, pictured above, fronted Chester Avenue on the opposite side of the block from the store.

Fashion shows were a frequent event at Higbee's and many of the other stores. Sometimes staged by Higbee's, other times by various area civic groups, the events were well attended and well publicized in the local media. This event in 1958 is in the Higbee's auditorium, which was located on the 10th floor of the building.

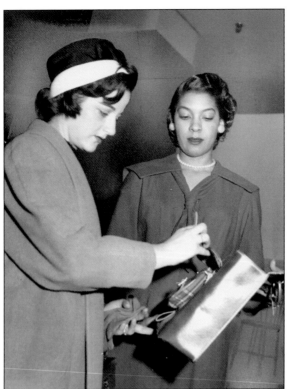

Sterling-Lindner employee Ms. Russell assists a customer with a purse that is for sale around 1959.

The 10th floor of Higbee's was the location of the culinary favorite the Silver Grille. The restaurant, a Higbee's original, was known from east side to west side for its elegance, fine food, and creative ways to serve children's meals. Children's food was served in a pretend stove, with the main course of food in the oven. Later children's meals were served in miniature Higbee's delivery trucks.

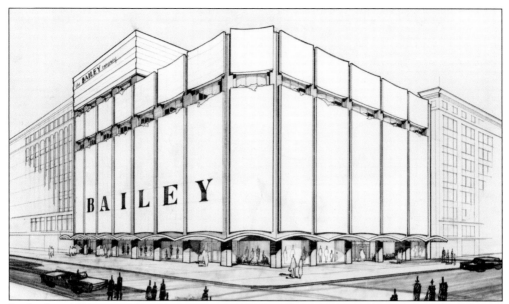

In the late 1950s, an architect was commissioned to design a new and "improved" look for the Bailey's flagship store. The original exterior, which had not changed to any large extent since the store was built in 1907–1910, was considered by management to be outdated, and a freshening up would bring the store into the 1950s. The facade (including most of the windows) was covered to give the building a uniform, cubed look, with the Bailey name featured prominently on Ontario Avenue.

Halle's frequently held import bazaars, featuring various products from different countries of origin. The events allowed Clevelanders to get a taste of the more exotic offerings from around the globe. For this particular import bazaar in 1959, Halle's set up a café on the outside sidewalk to satiate the hunger of excited shoppers.

The Cleveland Union Terminal Complex is shown, with Higbee's as the large rectangular building at the left base. (Library of Congress Historic American Buildings Survey.)

Higbee's, being locally owned, was well known for its activities in the community. Pictured above is the 18th annual art exhibition of the Cleveland Public School art instructors at the Higbee Gallery. At this particular event in 1962 there were 217 paintings, sculptures, and other art objects on display, all created by Cleveland Public Schools' art teachers.

A salesman assists a customer in selecting just the right suit at Higbee's.

Contrary to the modern incarnation of the department store, the Cleveland stores of the past truly offered a vast array of products for purchase. When reminiscing about favorite features of Higbee's, Halle's, the May Company, or the like, an often overlooked area is Halle's wine shop. Although alcoholic beverages are now limited mostly to grocery stores and specialty retailers, at the time Halle's wine shop offered a selection of wines to satiate even the pickiest connoisseur's taste.

A crowd waits to walk north across Euclid Avenue in front of the May Company building in the 1950s.

Richard Gurian and George Woodling (right) keep a tight grip on a Rembrandt original painting while Mr. and Mrs. William Holmes look on. They were all on hand, picture included, for the Guenther Art Gallery sale at the May Company store downtown in May 1963. The Guenther Art Gallery, dating back to 1863, was the premier source of art for the cultured set in Cleveland for nearly 100 years. Guenther's reign ended when the May Company purchased the gallery's entire collection, culminating in the headline-making exhibition and sale seen above.

Three

FACES BEHIND THE GLITTER

Although the store itself often gets the focus, nothing happened without the collective will of the management and employees behind the facades. Department stores in Cleveland were made up of tight-knit groups of employees led by management who lived in the community they served. Stores took great pride in their employees, recognizing longtime service—10, 25, 35, even 50 years of employment at a single store for some employees—with sincere gratitude, be it by a ceremony, gifts of government bonds, company-paid trips around the globe, or a combination. But one did not have to acquire years of service to get to shake hands with the captains of the ship; Halle's, for instance, held annual "coffee chats" where each and every employee had a chance to sit down with a hot cup of coffee and chat face to face with the big bosses, such as Samuel or Walter Halle. Stores also encouraged extracurricular endeavors for employees, with company athletic teams and artistic groups among the many activities available. Whatever the situation, Cleveland's department stores reflected an era when captains of commerce and industry lived in the communities where they did business and supported a "home-away-from-home" mentality for their employees.

The upper echelon of Halle's management poses for a photograph in 1949. Pictured are J. Henry Dippel, vice president and general superintendent.; Samuel H. Halle, chairman of the board (seated); Walter M. Halle, president (standing behind Samuel); Jay Iglauer, executive vice president and controller; Herbert S. Moorehouse, member of the board of directors; and A. E. Jacques, vice president and general merchandise manager.

One of the most enduring memories of Halle's commitment to its employees is the annual coffee chat. The sessions were a way to let the president of the company become acquainted with most (if not all) employees, and vice versa, with the ice broken over a hot cup of coffee. The events, conducted yearly, were one of the store's most enduring traditions, having originated in the early 20th century. At left, then president Walter Halle assists Betty Goldstein with sugaring her coffee while Lillian O'Donnell looks on around 1960.

With the department stores' concentration of local workers, it was frequent that employee get-togethers occurred. The May Company's 1948 Autumn Jamboree was one such event, with a turnout of over 7,500 of the area May Company staff at an energized Cleveland Public Hall downtown. The event featured various events, such as games, dancing, competitions, and raffles. Four lucky ladies posed with the "man of the hour": in front (from left to right) are Ethel Wagner and Betty Lipstreu, in the rear are Frances Marsh and Mrs. Ora Stone.

Sylvia Tester (left) and Jean Easterday (right), both Bailey's employees, pose with a Bailey's anniversary sale sign in 1953.

A Leaf from our Policy

MANY OF US ARE confronted by the necessity of deciding on matters that arise in the daily routine of business, not covered by the "Rules and Regulations." For helpful aid in such cases, remember one thing: This establishment puts no premium on clever tricks or cute business practice. Be open, frank, above all, Honest. Decide on the simple law of right or wrong—then you can't go wrong.

The Halle Bros. Co.

Honesty and integrity were of utmost importance to Halle's management, and it reflected in their policies and practices with employees. Walter (left) and Samuel Halle hold a plaque reading, "A Leaf from our Policy," which sums up the business practices of the Halle Brothers Company: "Many of us are confronted by the necessity of deciding on matters that arise in the daily routine of business not covered by the 'Rules and Regulations.' For helpful aid in such cases, remember one thing: This establishment puts no premium on clever tricks or cute business practice. Be open, frank, above all, Honest. Decide on the simple law of right or wrong—then you can't go wrong."

Like many employers of the time, Higbee's held employee picnics at various local locations. The get-togethers usually involved food and games and allowed employees, management, and their children to interact and generally have a good time outside the workplace. This picnic in 1934 was held at Wildwood Park on Cleveland's east side, a popular spot located just off Lake Erie.

Whereas it would be unthinkable today, part of the festivities at the 1934 Higbee Company employee picnic at Wildwood Park was a beauty pageant for the female staff. The five ladies pictured above were entrants in the contest, although it was not noted if any of them took the prize.

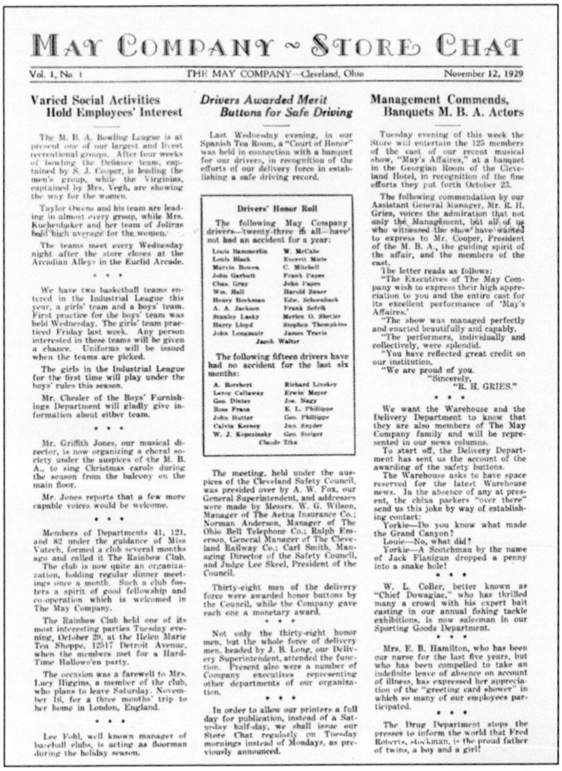

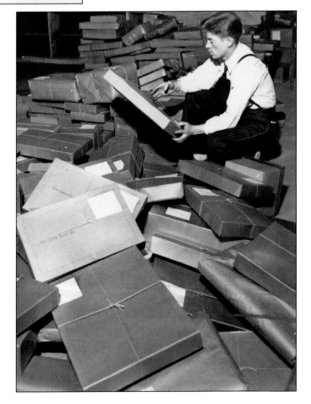

MAY COMPANY ~ STORE CHAT

Vol. 1, No. 1 — THE MAY COMPANY—Cleveland, Ohio — November 12, 1929

Varied Social Activities Hold Employees' Interest

The M. B. A. Bowling League is at present one of our largest and livest recreational groups. After four weeks of bowling the Defiance team, captained by S. J. Cooper, is leading the men's group, while the Virginias, captained by Mrs. Vegh, are showing the way for the women.

Taylor Owens and his team are leading in almost every group, while Mrs. Kuchenbaker and her team of Joliras hold high average for the women.

The teams meet every Wednesday night after the store closes at the Arcadian Alleys in the Euclid Arcade.

* * *

We have two basketball teams entered in the Industrial League this year, a girls' team and a boys' team. First practice for the boys' team was held Wednesday. The girls' team practiced Friday last week. Any person interested in these teams will be given a chance. Uniforms will be issued when the teams are picked.

The girls in the Industrial League for the first time will play under the boys' rules this season.

Mr. Chesler of the Boys' Furnishings Department will gladly give information about either team.

* * *

Mr. Griffith Jones, our musical director, is now organizing a choral society under the auspices of the M. B. A., to sing Christmas carols during the season from the balcony on the main floor.

Mr. Jones reports that a few more capable voices would be welcome.

* * *

Members of Departments 41, 121, and 82 under the guidance of Miss Vatech, formed a club several months ago and called it The Rainbow Club.

The club is now quite an organization, holding regular dinner meetings once a month. Such a club fosters a spirit of good fellowship and co-operation which is welcomed in The May Company.

The Rainbow Club held one of its most interesting parties Tuesday evening, October 29, at the Helen Marie Tea Shoppe, 12517 Detroit Avenue, when the members met for a Hard-Time Hallowe'en party.

The occasion was a farewell to Mrs. Lucy Higgins, a member of the club, who plans to leave Saturday, November 16, for a three months' trip to her home in London, England.

* * *

Lee Fohl, well known manager of baseball clubs, is acting as floorman during the holiday season.

Drivers Awarded Merit Buttons for Safe Driving

Last Wednesday evening, in our Spanish Tea Room, a "Court of Honor" was held in connection with a banquet for our drivers, in recognition of the efforts of our delivery force in establishing a safe driving record.

Drivers' Honor Roll

The following May Company drivers—twenty-three in all—have not had an accident for a year:

Louis Hammerlin	W. McCabe
Louis Black	Everett Miele
Marvin Bowen	C. Mitchell
John Garbutt	Frank Papes
Chas. Gray	John Papes
Wm. Hall	Harold Sauer
Henry Heckman	Edw. Schoenbeck
A. A. Jackson	Frank Sefcik
Stanley Lasky	Merlen O. Shetler
Harry Lloyd	Stephen Thompkins
John Longmuir	James Travis
Jacob Walter	

The following fifteen drivers have had no accident for the last six months:

A. Borchert	Richard Linskey
Leroy Callaway	Erwin Meyer
Geo. Dister	Jos. Nagy
Ross Frasa	E. L. Phillippe
John Hutter	Geo. Phillippe
Calvin Kerney	Jno. Snyder
W. J. Kopezinsky	Geo. Steiger
Claude Ziha	

The meeting, held under the auspices of the Cleveland Safety Council, was presided over by A. W. Fox, our General Superintendent, and addresses were made by Messrs. W. G. Wilson, Manager of The Aetna Insurance Co.; Norman Anderson, Manager of The Ohio Bell Telephone Co.; Ralph Emerson, General Manager of The Cleveland Railway Co.; Carl Smith, Managing Director of the Safety Council, and Judge Lee Skeel, President of the Council.

Thirty-eight men of the delivery force were awarded honor buttons by the Council, while the Company gave each one a monetary award.

* * *

Not only the thirty-eight honor men, but the whole force of delivery men, headed by J. B. Long, our Delivery Superintendent, attended the function. Present also were a number of Company executives representing other departments of our organization.

* * *

In order to allow our printers a full day for publication, instead of a Saturday half-day, we shall issue our Store Chat regularly on Tuesday mornings instead of Mondays, as previously announced.

Management Commends, Banquets M. B. A. Actors

Tuesday evening of this week the Store will entertain the 125 members of the cast of our recent musical show, "May's Affaires," at a banquet in the Georgian Room of the Cleveland Hotel, in recognition of the fine efforts they put forth October 23.

The following commendation by our Assistant General Manager, Mr. R. H. Gries, voices the admiration that not only the Management, but all of us who witnessed the show have wanted to express to Mr. Cooper, President of the M. B. A., the guiding spirit of the affair, and the members of the cast.

The letter reads as follows:

"The Executives of The May Company wish to express their high appreciation to you and the entire cast for its excellent performance of 'May's Affaires.'

"The show was managed perfectly and enacted beautifully and capably.

"The performers, individually and collectively, were splendid.

"You have reflected great credit on our institution.

"We are proud of you.

"Sincerely,
"R. H. GRIES."

* * *

We want the Warehouse and the Delivery Department to know that they are also members of The May Company family and will be represented in our news columns.

To start off, the Delivery Department has sent us the account of the awarding of the safety buttons.

The Warehouse asks to have space reserved for the latest Warehouse news. In the absence of any at present, the china packers "over there" send us this joke by way of establishing contact:

Yorkie—Do you know what made the Grand Canyon?

Louie—No, what did?

Yorkie—A Scotchman by the name of Jack Flanigan dropped a penny into a snake hole!

* * *

W. L. Coller, better known as "Chief Dowagiac," who has thrilled many a crowd with his expert bait casting in our annual fishing tackle exhibitions, is now salesman in our Sporting Goods Department.

* * *

Mrs. E. B. Hamilton, who has been our nurse for the last five years, but who has been compelled to take an indefinite leave of absence on account of illness, has expressed her appreciation of the "greeting card shower" in which so many of our employees participated.

* * *

The Drug Department stops the presses to inform the world that Fred Roberts, stockman, is the proud father of twins, a boy and a girl!

Several stores circulated newsletters for their employees, covering everything from operational information to notifications about company events and activities to employee birth announcements. Some of the notable newsletters include the May Company's *Store Chat* (pictured) and Halle's *Hallegram*.

A Halle's employee sorts through packages ready for delivery in December 1936. Deliverymen had nicknames for the different packages: large boxes were called "junk," while small boxes were called "small stuff."

Enthusiastic Bailey's employees enjoy themselves during a company party in 1936.

Hotel Cleveland was the location of the ceremony for the inductees into the Bailey Company Quarter Century Club. On this occasion, 21 employees were celebrated for their 25 years of service to the company. Aside from service pins and the notoriety of their longtime service, each employee also received government bonds, presented by Bailey's president Lambert Oppenheim (far right). With their induction, Bailey's counted 95 employees with 25 years of tenure.

While many people automatically think of the sales floor when department stores are discussed, there are many back-office workers who make the stores operate as they should. The Higbee Company was no different; it maintained a large staff of clerical, maintenance, warehouse, and other back-office workers. This photograph from 1935 offers a glimpse into one of the clerical offices at the Higbee Company. The staff is also entirely female, which was not unusual for the time period.

Much to the enjoyment of the little shoppers of Cleveland's families, the May Company expansion in 1931 also included an enhanced playroom for children. Shown standing on the merry-go-round with two children is Isabel White, the director of the playroom.

With token cigar in hand, Lambert G. Oppenheim welcomes his successor to the helm of the Bailey Company. Oppenheim, the retiring president of Bailey's (right), poses for a photograph with incoming president Harold W. Scher. The changing of the guard occurred in 1956.

Halle's was well known for being very employee friendly, with recognition for particular accomplishments or service marks. Celebrating her 50th year with the Halle Brothers Company is Anne Kunesh, who is being presented with her reward for her longtime service by Walter Halle. In addition to the tastefully decorated "50" cake and ceremony, Halle's treated Kunesh to a three-week tour of Europe, spanning 10 countries.

Gawkers and strikers congregate outside the entrance to Sterling and Welch in 1946. At the time, the company and employees were embroiled in a bitter labor dispute. Sterling and Welch, which specialized in furniture, was one of the predecessors of Sterling-Lindner-Davis.

For many years Halle's featured an elaborate system of vacuum tubes. Instead of processing monetary transactions on the sales floor as is standard today, cash and sales slips were sent back and forth via a pneumatic tube system to a centralized office in the building and back to the sales floor. Two women are seen above processing transactions via the system.

Higbee's executive Herbert Strawbridge (left) has a lighthearted chat with business rival Chisholm Halle, Halle's president, in 1967. Strawbridge, who would later become Higbee's president, was well known throughout Cleveland as an outstanding businessman and community philanthropist. Chisholm Halle was the youthful—and last—Halle who manned the helm of the retail empire, becoming president (due to the illness of his father, Walter) at just 33 years of age.

A group of businessmen involved with planning and constructing the Parmatown May Company store poses on August 21, 1960. From left to right are Sam Rosenburg, vice president and general manager of the May Company; Nathan Dauby, president of May's; Victor Gruen of Victor Gruen and Associates; and Francis Coy, vice president and assistant general manager of May's. Gruen was known for his design of enclosed shopping malls nationwide. Dauby spent more than half a century at the May Company of Cleveland, rising from the shoe department to president. He also was a community philanthropist.

During the first half of the 20th century, many things that are now made outside the store or even outside the country were routinely made either in-house or locally. Above, May Company employees Mildred Heffenle and Albina Gorenc make cream-covered cherries, by hand, for later sale at the store.

Santa Claus, by day known as Al Morton, gets his beard pulled by troublemaking new members of the May Company's 35 Year Club at a ceremony held at Hotel Carter in November 1958. From left to right, the beard puller is Mrs. Armin Leonhardt, followed by Mae McCaffery, Al Morton, Celia Laufman, and Louise Gallas.

John P. Murphy was a longtime associate of the Higbee Company. Murphy originally came to Cleveland at the behest of railroad magnates the Van Sweringen brothers, brought on board for his experience in railroad law. After the bankruptcy of the Van Sweringen empire (which included the Higbee Company), the store was bought out by Murphy and Van Sweringen associate Charles L. Bradley. Murphy returned to practicing law for several years but came to the store as president after Bradley's death in 1944. From then on Murphy was intertwined with Higbee's, becoming chief executive officer, a position that he held until 1967, and then honorary director until his death in 1969. His legacy carries on through the John P. Murphy Foundation, which continues to support various arts, education, and community-related causes, largely in the state of Ohio.

While this may appear to be a get-together of extras from the Barney Miller show, it is actually a group of employees hanging out in the May Company warehouse garage at East Forty-first Street and Payne Avenue. Nick Murray, a security guard for the May Company, is the only person identified in the photograph. He stands at center left with sunglasses.

The year 1980 brought the world the birth of Pac-Man, the death of John Lennon, and the perplexing question, "Who shot J. R.?" In Cleveland, it also brought H. Gene Nau, president and chief executive officer of the May Company of Ohio at the downtown store, stirring an omelet in a gigantic frying pan. In later years, Nau made the jump to Higbee's, serving as chairman and president.

Four

CELEBRITIES' HOME AWAY FROM HOME

Department stores' positions as the centers of community commerce lent them a special role when it came time for celebrities to reach out across the country to promote a new book, show, or movie. For much of the 20th century, it was not uncommon for celebrities to make promotional stops in major cities across the United States, and choice locations for these stops ultimately included the department stores. In this respect, Cleveland's department stores were no different, hosting the likes of many popular stars of the time, such as Lucille Ball, Rock Hudson, or even Charlton Heston.

While movies were only available in theaters, in the days before category-killer big-box stores, department stores were the hot spot to purchase books of all types. With that in mind, they were essential for authors touring the country to promote a new book. Some stores, such as Halle's and Higbee's, were known for their autograph parties, in which events coordinators would arrange for not one but two, three, five, or more authors to appear at once, creating quite a buzz—and a stampede of potential shoppers.

At other times, stores would arrange for celebrities or popular figures to appear in conjunction with a special promotion or area event, and many times they would pull notable people from the Cleveland area to appear. Such was the case with Halle's celebration of the 1960 Olympic Games, when Cleveland natives (and prior Olympic standouts) Harrison Dillard and Jesse Owens made an appearance.

Major department stores were truly a promotional boon to celebrities but also were a catalyst in drawing popular figures to Cleveland that would otherwise not have been in the area. It was a mutually beneficial arrangement to all involved and was yet another example of the positive role the stores played in the community.

Charlton Heston entertains fans as he autographs books at Higbee's in 1973. Well known for his long and storied acting career, Heston performed in modern-day classics such as *Ben Hur*, *Planet of the Apes*, and *The Ten Commandments*, among many others. In the heyday of the traditional department stores, it was not unusual for celebrities and other notable persons to be involved in store promotions or to make a stop on publicity tours.

Prince Georges Matchabelli, originally of the nation of Georgia, visited Halle's in 1934. Matchabelli and his wife, Norina, immigrated to the United States in 1921 following a hostile takeover of Georgia by Russia. The prince was a chemist and in 1924 founded the Prince Matchabelli Perfume Company, well known for its distinct, color-coded, crown-shaped perfume bottles, one of which can be seen in the woman's hand, at left. Although Prince Georges died in 1935, his line of perfumes, now owned by Unilever, continues to be sold in 2009.

May Company book buyer Angela Colagiovanni spends some quality time with screenwriter Robert W. Anderson and singer Mel Torme. Anderson was on hand to promote his new book *Getting Up and Going Home*, while Torme was promoting his new novel *Wynner*.

Ralph B. Pendery, executive vice president of Halle's, escorts film and stage star Ethel Merman. Merman, in town for the premiere of her movie *The Art of Love*, made an appearance at the official dedication of Halle's Alley. Halle's Alley was the portion of East Twelfth Street between Prospect Avenue and Huron Road that ran through the Halle's facilities.

Famous big band leader Tommy Dorsey shares the celebrity table with Halle's model Clyde Rickenbrode at the Halle's tearoom in 1955. Dorsey was well known nationally as a successful big band musician.

In October 1929, Halle's bookshop hosted well-known illustrator William (Willy) Pogany. Pogany, a native of Hungary, illustrated numerous books in the first half of the 20th century, many of which were based on classics such as *Red Ridinghood*, *Alice's Adventures in Wonderland*, and a retelling of Homer in *The Adventures of Odysseus and the Tale of Troy*. Although many of his books were children's, he also did some illustrations for adult publications and was a scene designer for the Metropolitan Opera House in New York. Pogany was at Halle's doing book signings for his book *Willy Pogany's Mother Goose*, which he both authored and illustrated.

Actress Zsa Zsa Gabor (center) poses for the camera with Nancy Anderson, Halle's public relations director, at Halle's in 1969.

In addition to celebrities of film, television, and the written word, clothing designers would occasionally make stops at major department stores as well. The year 1967 brought a visit to Halle's by clothing designer Bill Blass, who posed with (from left to right) Mrs. Warner Bishop and Mrs. Carl B. Stokes, wife of newly elected mayor of Cleveland, Carl B. Stokes. Blass, who died in 2002, still lives on in modern fashion via his namesake company, Bill Blass Limited.

Halle's hosted a book brunch with six authors in November 1966. From left to right are Robert McCloskey, author and illustrator of the children's book *Burt Dow: Deep Water Man*; Fletcher Knebel, *The Zinzin Road*; Louis B. Seltzer, longtime editor of the *Cleveland Press*, author of *Six and God*; Anita Loos, autobiographer of *A Girl Like I*; Halle's heiress, Kay Halle, author of *The Irrepressible Churchill*; and Bill Wamby (Bill Wambsganss), whose tales of being an early player in professional baseball appeared in *The Glory of Their Times*.

While many local stores were focusing on local media advertising and promotions, in 1955 Higbee's lured Miss Frances from the nationally broadcast television show *Ding Dong School* to its auditorium. Initially broadcast on NBC and later syndicated, the show was very popular with preschool-age children.

It was a standing-room-only crowd at Halle's for the visit of movie star and teenage heartthrob Rock Hudson in October 1959. Hudson was in the midst of a publicity tour for his new movie *Pillow Talk*, which he costarred in with actress Doris Day, and many in the audience had brought their *Pillow Talk* 45s to have autographed. The movie went on to be a blockbuster and a great success for the actor.

Lucille Ball visits Halle's in 1956. Aside from starring in her popular show *I Love Lucy*, in 1956 she also starred in the film *Forever, Darling*, a romantic comedy costarring (much like her show) her husband, Desi Arnaz.

The May Company brought in a few actors from the then-new movie *Grease 2* (1982) to sign autographs at its store downtown. At left are twins Liz and Jean Sagal, who played sorority girls in the film, and on the other end of the table is Bernie Hiller, who played the role of boy greaser. The Sagals are the younger sisters of Katey Sagal, Peggy Bundy on the show *Married . . . With Children*. Hiller is now an acting coach in Los Angeles.

A group gathers to pose with two popular authors in 1934. Seated is Bess Streeter Aldrich, a popular author and magazine writer. Her most recent book at the time was *Miss Bishop*, which in 1941 was made into a film called *Cheers to Miss Bishop*. On the far right with book in hand is author Sterling North. North was a successful novelist best remembered for his 1963 book *Rascal*. His most recent book at the time of this photograph was *Plowing on Sunday*.

Ozzie Nelson autographs his autobiography, *Ozzie*, for a fan at Higbee's in 1973. Nelson was perhaps best known for his role in *The Adventures of Ozzie and Harriet*, a long-running sitcom from the 1950s and 1960s. Aside from being the quintessential 1950s and 1960s family sitcom, the show was unique in that his family on the show—wife Harriet, and sons, David and Ricky—were also his family in real life.

In celebration of the 1960s Olympic Games, Higbee's invited several 1936 Berlin Olympic champions to visit. On the left, Harrison Dillard, four-time gold medalist and talented hurdler, attended East Tech High School and Baldwin-Wallace College. In the middle, Pat McCormick also won four Olympic gold medals in diving. On the right, Cleveland favorite Jesse Owens, four-time gold medalist in track, also attended East Tech High School and Ohio State University.

Gerty Desjardin and Richard Dwyer give their culinary skills a try—if only symbolically. Desjardin and Dwyer were well known as performers in the traveling ice-skating performances of Ice Follies, similar to Ice Capades.

Halle's heiress Kay Halle sits with Ann Richards for this 1954 photograph. Kay Halle was something of a celebrity herself. Professionally she was an accomplished journalist and writer, and personally she was associated in both a friendly and romantic capacity with many famous names of the time. She counted among her associates George Gershwin, Winston Churchill's son Randolph (who reportedly proposed to her; she declined), Buckminster Fuller, and many others. Upon her death in 1997, her national prominence warranted a summary article of her life in the *New York Times*.

Five

CHRISTMASTIME WINDOWS, KEYS, AND GIANT TREES

While downtown shopping was always an event, shopping Cleveland's department stores during the holiday season was truly a sight to behold. Many things, such as the elaborate Christmas display windows, were fantastic but not unique to Cleveland. However, Cleveland was home to several holiday festivities that were not—and in many cases, could not—be duplicated elsewhere.

Perhaps the best-known Christmas tree in Ohio (and to hear some people tell it, in the United States) was undoubtedly the mammoth tree found at Sterling-Lindner. Starting with a relatively reasonable two-story tree in 1927, Sterling and Welch, predecessor to Sterling-Lindner, continually attempted to outdo itself each year with successively grand, and successively massive, trees. By 1967, the final Christmas that Sterling-Lindner set up the giant tree, the Christmas tree had grown to over 70 feet in height and was covered in over 2,500 giant Christmas ornaments.

The other uniquely Cleveland Christmas tradition to originate with its department stores was Mr. Jingeling, found for most of his career on the seventh floor of Halle's. Mr. Jingeling, Santa's locksmithing elf, originated as a onetime promotion for the store back in 1956. Since then, Mr. Jingeling has been a holiday tradition played by several characters over the years. Perhaps most impressive is that Mr. Jingeling has outlived Halle's, the store that originated him.

When combined with the slush and snow that dominates northeast Ohio winters, the holiday festivities shared in the grand opulence of Cleveland's department stores have made indelible memories for several generations of Clevelanders.

Charles Dickens's classic tale A *Christmas Carol* is depicted in this Christmas season window of the Halle's on Euclid Avenue.

No strings! Magically floating above the table, the doll assistant gracefully allows the doll magician to levitate her. This scene was part of the Christmas 1980 window display at Halle's.

Bill Barrett gets dressed up for his stint as Santa Claus at Halle's in 1955. This was the last year before the introduction of the perpetually popular and exclusively Halle's figure Mr. Jingeling.

Santa Claus (better known as Bill Barret) entertains the Christmas wishes of Halle's shopper Kathy Halligan.

A group of women browses the jewelry counter at Halle's in December 1930. Although the effects of the Depression were already being felt, department stores provided a welcome respite of holiday cheer during the Christmas season.

Christmas cards galore cover the table at Halle's. The massive amount of Christmas cards was on sale as part of the day-after-Christmas sale at the store in 1955.

Many times, the Christmas decorations inside the stores were as exciting as the display windows outside. In 1953, Halle's featured a child-sized toy soldier display that could be seen from the upper balcony.

An old-fashioned Christmas sleigh ride is depicted in this Halle's window. Many windows, aside from being well crafted, were also animated.

Christmas was a special time in Cleveland, and none was more special than at Halle's. Weary shoppers relax overlooking the sales floor during the Christmas season of 1963. The sign on the right is touting Halle's new wine shop.

The May Company is crawling with customers on the day after Christmas in 1967. While many were returning gifts that did not fit or were not wanted, many others were enjoying the half-off sale of Christmas goods. May's basement store was known throughout the year for fantastic bargains that all customers could enjoy.

A sure sign that the Christmas season had begun was the arrival of the giant Christmas tree at Sterling-Lindner. Often reputed to be one of the largest Christmas trees in the country, the tradition originated in 1927 with the Sterling and Welch Company, a predecessor of Sterling-Lindner. In varying heights and weights over the years, the Sterling-Lindner tree was without a doubt the most notable Christmas tree in Cleveland.

Over time, the Sterling-Lindner store lineage repeatedly topped itself for having the tallest indoor Christmas tree. For example, the 1933 Christmas tree at Sterling and Welch (seen at left) barely reached the top of the second floor and was less than impressive in girth. By 1950, the resident Christmas tree for the season had grown to 50 feet tall, and in 1954, Sterling featured the "biggest ever" tree at 54 feet tall; while in 1960, the *Cleveland Press* reported Sterling featured "what may be the largest Christmas tree in the world" at 60 feet. The 1966 tree, seen below, stretched to a whopping 73 feet and again was reported by the *Cleveland Press* as "the tallest in the 39 years the store has had the display."

The Sterling-Lindner tree was a massive endeavor. Although the exact figures varied from tree to tree and year to year, the approximate statistics were as follows: 2,500 one-foot-wide ornaments, 1,200 yards of tinsel, 60 pounds of tinfoil icicles, 25 gallons of water per day, and six inches of growth of the tree inside the store. (Cleveland Public Library Photograph Collection.)

While the stores were always festive during Christmastime, the streets outside were joyful as well. At the intersection of Euclid Avenue and Huron Road, the Halle Brothers building looks down on holiday wreaths strung up and down the city blocks for Christmas 1936.

Much like its larger competition, Sterling and Welch also offered attractions for the children of its patrons. The Christmas of 1949 brought a very popular carousel, which, as seen in this picture, was operating at full capacity.

At 25 feet tall, Santa towers in front of the then-new May Company store at Parmatown Shopping Center. While not as grand as the Christmas displays at the flagship department stores downtown, noticeable effort was made to celebrate the holidays at the suburban stores as well. As retailing consolidated into regional and then national chains, most of the traditional holiday extravagance was discontinued.

The holiday season of 1948 ushered in Christmas windows at the new Shaker Square Halle's. The window space was considerably smaller than those at the Halle's in Playhouse Square but festive nonetheless.

The first Christmas on the Moon took place in one of Halle's store windows during the Christmas of 1967. The 1960s was a time of great interest in space exploration as the United States challenged the USSR for dominance in the field. As such, the space theme was capitalized on by many areas of media and retail, with Cleveland retailers being no different.

Sterling-Lindner may have had the most renowned giant Christmas tree in town, but in 1968, the Higbee's tree in the Cleveland Union Terminal lobby would have to do. Earlier that year, Sterling-Lindner shut its doors for good, leaving all of Cleveland to mourn the loss of the annual monster Christmas tree it was so well known for. Nevertheless, at 50 feet, the Higbee tree was nothing to sneeze at and filled the giant Christmas tree role well.

A Christmas window display at Higbee's is staged as a scene from *The Nutcracker*. The window displays were for many years considered essential points of advertising for Cleveland retailers. Each year, the major department stores would attempt to outdo each other's displays with elaborate setups and themes. While the windows no doubt assisted in drawing in customers from the streets outside, they also allowed for a certain amount of bragging rights for the store with the best display.

Like its larger retail neighbors, Bailey's took part in the Christmas display window fun just the same.

Faux bells adorn the interior arches of the Higbee Company. The holiday-accented arches provide contrast to allow for the proper perspective of the cavernous sales floor in the store.

Customers crowd the sales floor at Higbee's in 1973. One holiday favorite at Higbee's, at least for children, was the Twigbee Shop. The Twigbee Shop was a store within the children's department—for children only—where they could purchase affordable gifts for their parents and other family members.

Perhaps one of the few holiday characters to usurp Santa Claus in popularity, if only in Cleveland, was Halle's Mr. Jingeling. Mr. Jingeling, as the story goes, was a key-making elf who saved Christmas one holiday season when Santa lost the keys to his Treasure House of Toys. Jingeling fashioned new keys for Santa, who was thus able to gain access to the toys and carry on with Christmas gift giving. As a reward for saving Christmas for all the good girls and boys, Mr. Jingeling was made the official "keeper of the keys," which he always had in hand at all his appearances. Boys and girls who visited him also got their very own cardboard key that opened Santa's Treasure House of Toys. (Photograph by William G. Vorpe, Cleveland Public Library Photograph Collection.)

Mr. Jingeling was originally the invention of Frank Jacobi, an advertising agent from Chicago and an associate of Walter Halle. Mr. Jingeling was created as a clever onetime holiday promotion of Halle's for Christmas 1956. However, the response was so strong that Mr. Jingeling was made an annual promotion for the store, which lasted beyond the store's eventual closing in 1982.

Max Ellis, an actor from the Playhouse Theater, played as the original Mr. Jingeling for television appearances on Channel 5's *Captain Penny Show*, while Cleveland police officer Tom Moviel filled the role for in-store appearances. Ellis continued his role as the television Mr. Jingeling through 1964, ending with his sudden death that year. The picture at right shows Ellis in the role of detective in the Playhouse Theater's production of *Angel Street* in 1944.

After Max Ellis's untimely demise in 1964, Karl Mackey took over the Mr. Jingeling role for 1965. Mackey also had a background in performance, as he was the managing director of the Lakewood Little Theatre. However, Mackey found the role to be too time consuming when combined with his duties at the theater and relinquished it after only one season. (Photograph by Marvin M. Greene, Cleveland Public Library Photograph Collection.)

After Mackey's resignation as Mr. Jingeling, the character was taken over by Earl Keyes, who is most often cited as *the* Mr. Jingeling. Keyes was no stranger to acting, having been a longtime producer, director, and actor at WEWS Channel 5. From 1966 until his death in 2000, Keyes played the part of Mr. Jingeling, eventually surpassing the store that originated the character—Halle's. After Halle's closed in 1982, Keyes (as Mr. Jingeling) moved to Higbee's 10th floor and later to Tower City.

Mr. Jingeling is carried on for the next generation of Cleveland children by Jonathon Wilhelm of Traditions Alive in Lakewood. Wilhelm has made appearances as Mr. Jingeling across the Cleveland area, including a special "Mr. Jingeling's Holiday Express" aboard the Cuyahoga Valley Scenic Railroad. (Copyright Janet Macoska, courtesy of Traditions Alive Company, LLC.)

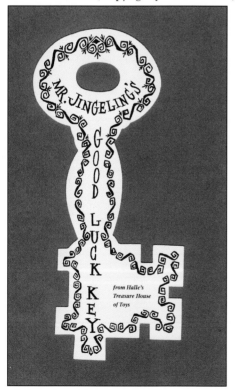

For decades, children visiting Mr. Jingeling would receive cardboard keys of their own to unlock Santa's Treasure House of Toys. (Copyright Janet Macoska, courtesy of Traditions Alive Company, LLC.)

Even today, many Clevelanders can still recall the jingle that Mr. Jingeling would recite: "Mister Jingeling / How you tingling / Keeper of the keys / On Halle's seventh floor / We'll be looking for / You to turn the keys / He keeps track / Of Santa's sack / And Treasure House of Toys / With wind up things / That Santa brings / To all good girls and boys." (Copyright Mort Tucker Photography.)

For decades the department store Christmas displays entertained Clevelanders young and old. Here children admire the windows at Higbee's.

During the days of downtown shopping, each department store would keep a staff of set designers to create any special sets of displays it might need, which included the exciting window displays at Christmas. Shown above is Halle's special events designer Ron Newell (at left) with Mrs. Walter Kelley and Mrs. Peter Galvin.

Even during the Great Depression, the Christmas festivities still went on at Cleveland's retailers. This 1934 photograph depicts a giant Christmas tree with carolers on an elevated platform outside Higbee's.

Fatigued clerk Shirley Bryan advises John MacArthur on just the right perfume as a gift for his wife. MacArthur was making his last-minute purchase at Halle's on Christmas Eve 1953. December 24, then as now, culminated in a rush of last-minute shoppers looking for a gift for that special someone, as evidenced by the disarray behind the counter and Bryan's shoeless feet.

The May Company facade is seen with decorations for the Christmas season of 1956. Aside from the typical holiday lighting and display windows, the store also featured trees on the sidewalk overhang and a light-up Santa in a sleigh, with a crew of reindeer "flying" up the front of the building. (Cleveland Public Library Photograph Collection.)

Nothing says "sale" like the basement at the May Company the day after Christmas. In 1964, the young ladies above are eagerly looking through the half-price Christmas cards, no longer needed for this season but just fine for the next year.

Perfume for the special someone at home was as popular in 1931 as it is now. The fragrance counter at Halle's is depicted bustling with pre-Christmas activity in December of that year.

Alice in Wonderland was depicted in displays in Halle's Christmas World Fantasyland Animated Maze located in the seventh-floor lounge in 1977.

Two women look over the holiday traditions display windows at Halle's, which were featured during Christmas 1971. The particular window in question describes the Italian legend of La Befana, an old woman who flies on a broom and brings stockings full of presents to the children of Italy each January 6.

A packed sales floor greats customers of Higbee's during the Christmas season of 1963. The store was similarly adorned nearly 20 years later when the cult classic film A Christmas Story was filmed there in 1982.

Six

BECKONING CALL OF THE SUBURBS

Following World War II, it became apparent that new opportunities for expansion for Cleveland's department stores had arisen in the suburbs. New housing for the country's returning servicemen and their families was soon complemented with new retail development. Although some of the earlier stores, such as Halle's Cedar Center and Shaker Square locations, were but a fraction of the size of the downtown sites, it was more convenient for suburban families to drive a short distance and park—for free—as opposed to braving the trek to Euclid Avenue by car, on the bus, or on the rapid.

By the 1950s, suburban stores had grown in size, with some locations like May's in University Heights shooting to two or even three stories of shopping. Others, like Bailey's Lakeshore Plaza store in Euclid, were the anchor stores for another innovation—strip malls. Again, ample free parking and a short drive was a big draw to these significant, albeit scaled down, stores.

As the conservative 1950s turned into the progressive 1960s, the draw of suburban shopping was having a significant negative impact on the big stores on Euclid Avenue. But suburbanization was by then an unstoppable force, and many of the major stores continued to build farther and farther outward, even beyond Cuyahoga County itself. Full-scale enclosed shopping malls arrived in the Cleveland area with the opening of Severance Center Mall in Cleveland Heights in 1963, with Halle's and Higbee's shoring up either end of the mall. From that point on, malls were the project of choice for Cleveland's largest department stores, with Halle's, Higbee's, and the May Company expanding prolifically into the suburbs and beyond, to Lorain, Lake, Summit, and Stark Counties. Expansion continued with newer and larger malls being constructed into the 1970s.

During this time period convenience trumped opulence, and smaller stores in consumers' backyards became the model over having one massive store located downtown. As is the rule in retail, when the consumers speak, the stores listen.

With great foresight, Bailey's ushered in the era of suburban shopping with the opening of its east side store at Euclid Avenue and East 101st Street in 1929. Although decidedly urban today, at the time the neighborhood was considered to be on the fringe for a department store location. The move was an attempt to provide a convenient outlet to those now living that far from the center of the city.

The Bailey Company continued its expansion into the suburbs with the 1930 opening of its Lakewood store at Detroit Avenue and Warren Road. This store balanced its representation in the city and inner-ring suburbs, mirroring the east side store opened the year before.

Although Halle's had established satellite stores in different markets such as Erie, Pennsylvania, in 1929, and Canton, in 1930, it was not until the late 1940s that it began to move toward suburbanization. This 1950 photograph shows the small Cedar Center store located on the University Heights–Cleveland Heights border.

Shaker Square represented one of Halle's first forays into traditional suburban branch stores. Opened in 1948, the store brought a sample of Halle's goods to the upscale neighborhoods in Shaker Heights and the eastern edge of Cleveland. Planned by architect Robert A. Little, the building was well received and won several awards for design. In 2005, the building was added to the National Register of Historic Places for both its significance as an example of international-style architecture as well as its place in Cleveland retail history.

Despite the cold weather, customers flocked to the new Bailey's store on Lakeshore Boulevard at East 228th Street. By the 1950s, stores such as Bailey's had begun moving into the new retailing concept of the time period, strip malls. With a location closer to middle-class suburban shoppers and ample parking for the family car, the plazas were a welcome reprieve from trips downtown to congested Euclid Avenue.

The Bailey Company anchored the new Lakeshore Plaza in Euclid at Lakeshore Boulevard and East 228th Street. Strip plazas were a new convenience, with ample parking—in this case, 1,000 parking spaces—compared to downtown shopping. The added attraction to the ample parking was that there was no charge for making use of it.

By 1955, when other stores were just beginning to make inroads into the suburbs, Bailey's had been in Lakewood long enough to necessitate a remodel of the building. The street-level display windows were reduced in size, and a polished rose granite exterior was added to the front of the store. Inside the store was redesigned to follow the trend of allowing customers to browse and select goods themselves, as opposed to keeping most merchandise behind counters.

The new Southland Shopping Center in Middleburg Heights provided the perfect location for Halle's to extend itself into the southwest suburbs. The store building, like the plaza itself, was (and as of 2009, still is) owned by Anthoni Visconsi and Associates, a pioneer in construction of the suburban shopping plaza. The two-level store was designed by architects Matzinger and Grosel and slated to be completed by 1958.

At over 353,000 square feet, May's on the Heights, was one of the largest suburban department stores of any of the local chains. It featured four levels in the main section (lighter-colored square, left) and nine levels in the customer service section (taller, dark section, right). The store was well known for the bell hanging from a circular structure at the corner of Cedar and Warrensville Center Roads (lower left-hand corner). Operating for nearly five decades, the store (then named Kaufmann's) was rebuilt as part of the new University Square Shopping Center in 2003.

A troupe of suburb dwellers crowds the front of the building for the presentation of the new May Company store at Warrensville Center and Cedar Roads in University Heights. The store opened on November 1, 1957.

Robert Gries (left), manager of the May's on the Heights store, reviews receipts from the sports department with William Reith.

In keeping with the theme of imitating their "big sisters" downtown, the suburban stores were made to have similar features, at first. The Geranium Room at the Halle's store at Severance approximated the quality eating available at the flagship store on Euclid Avenue.

The cutting-edge cash register at the new May Company store at Parmatown Shopping Center allows for a different point of view of the term *desktop*. Jacqueline Lyons (far right), training chief for the May Company, gives new hires instruction on how to operate the great machine in preparation for the store opening in 1960. Trainees pictured are (from left to right) Leona Rygielski, Pat Oberst, Marie Paine, and Margaret Rots.

The ceremonial dirt is shoveled at the groundbreaking of the May Company at Parmatown Shopping Center.

Herman Myers, the manager of the Bailey Company's Eastgate store in Mayfield Heights, pumps up his sales force in 1960. The store was slated to have its grand opening later that morning, and the staff needed to prepare to capitalize on, and deal with, the predicted onslaught of eager shoppers. In addition to the eager staff, a clown was also on hand to entertain.

May's new store at Parmatown Shopping Center is shown shortly after opening in 1960. The center would later be roofed over and turned into an enclosed mall.

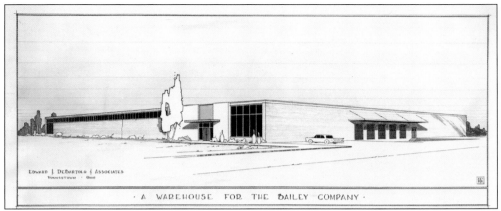

By the middle of the century, retail stores were not the only thing moving to the suburbs. The architectural drawing above, made in 1960, depicts the new warehouse for the Bailey Company, to be built in Walton Hills near the Ford Motors plant. The building was to be built and owned by shopping mall magnate Edward J. Debartolo's company and leased back to Bailey's.

When Westgate Center opened in 1954, Halle's was the premier anchor. The two-level store was a shift in suburban design for the chain, whose prior suburban stores had been relatively small endeavors. Even so, the Westgate store was still undersized in comparison to the downtown store, which remained the focal point during the 1950s. The trend toward larger, multiple-level suburban stores continued on into the future. The Halle's at Westgate added a third level to the store in 1969.

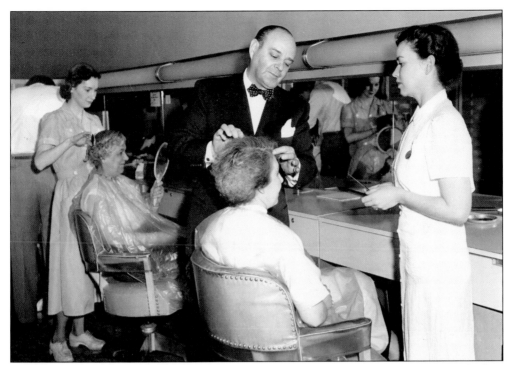

Salons were also a feature found downtown that were transported to many of the suburban stores. Above, Halle's stylists train at the new Westgate store salon.

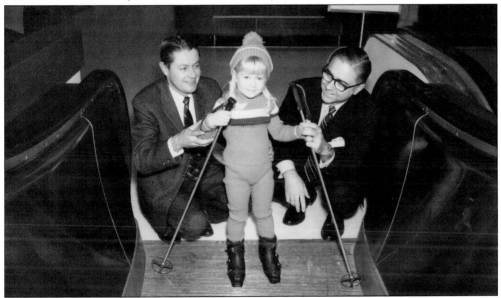

In November 1969, the new third floor at Halle's opened at Westgate Mall. The extra level provided an additional 50,000 square feet to the already-substantial store, making it the largest suburban Halle's in the chain. Celebrating this exciting turn of events is Fairview Park mayor Charles Mooney (left), store manager Rudy Flock (right), and Flock's four-year-old daughter Karen. They are preparing to take the inaugural trip on the escalator to the new floor, which featured home furnishings and sporting goods.

Walter Halle and associates look over the plans for the soon-to-be-built Severance Center Mall in Cleveland Heights in April 1962. Halle's was to be a leading anchor of the project, with Higbee's shoring up the other end of the shopping center. Severance Center was part of a new innovation in retailing, building on the successful strip mall concept; it was the first enclosed shopping mall in the region. The Severance moniker was used as the project was built on the former John L. Severance estate.

Remnants of John L. Severance's Longwood estate were still visible after the commercial development of the property into Severance Center. In the parking lot near Higbee's was a marble fountain that survived. When Severance Center was redeveloped into an open-air shopping center, the local historical society had the fountain moved closer to Mayfield Road, thus ensuring the fountain not only survived beyond the estate but beyond Higbee's and the mall as well.

Eventually the department stores spread their territory throughout the region. Higbee's, the May Company, and Halle's opened or acquired stores in Canton, Elyria, Mentor, and Akron, among others. For Halle's, this harkened back to earlier days when it had satellite stores in Canton, Mansfield, Warren, and Erie and New Castle, Pennsylvania. Above, the Halle's at Summit Mall in Fairlawn is pictured.

The North Olmsted May Company store featured three levels, which made it larger than many other suburban stores. The store was built to complement a plaza that was already on the west side of the site. Great Northern Mall was built on the east side of the lot several years later, using the May Company store as an anchor.

Throughout the 1960s and 1970s, the new Higbee Company stores built as anchors to local enclosed shopping malls varied little in appearance. This picture from 1966 of the new Higbee's store at Midway Mall in Elyria looks much the same as stores built 10 years later. Even in the 21st century, the design—particularly the ripple-topped columns at the entrances—gives away the locations of stores that used to bear the Higbee's name.

The May Company at Parmatown sparkles in 1968. Although the outlying stores were, to varying degrees, scaled back from their downtown counterparts, management still attempted to maintain a sense of the downtown shopping experience. At the Parmatown May Company, large chandeliers hung from the mall entrance and across the sales floor ceiling.

In the mid-1970s, all three remaining major department stores (the May Company of Cleveland, Higbee's, and Halle's) had the opportunity to be in the largest enclosed shopping mall in the country at the time: Randall Park Mall in North Randall. Initial renderings of the mall had all three of the local group (Halle's is to the left of JCPenney; Higbee's is to the right; and the May Company is above that); however, only Higbee's and the May Company would end up being built. It was reported that Halle's financial difficulties and subsequent closure led to the option never being exercised.

Higbee's court at Euclid Square Mall is packed with onlookers during the debut of the shopping center in February 1977.

Like the downtown stores before them, eventually the suburban stores would be remodeled to varying degrees. The May Company store at Parmatown was updated to 1970s standards, which meant, among other things, mirrored paneling and a revised logo.

Like the rest of the chain, the Halle's at Severance Center was shuttered in 1982. The closure of the chain left gaps in shopping centers across the region but was particularly difficult for Severance Center; the space remained vacant for another seven years before being occupied by Pittsburgh's Joseph Horne Company.

Seven

ONLY THE
STRONG SURVIVE

From the 1960s on, the downtown locations of Cleveland's department stores accelerated a downward slide as customers were lost to suburban stores. A scenario that had been sheer speculation in the 1950s had quickly become a reality for retailers of the day. Initially, many of the stores continued to attempt to attract shoppers to their downtown stores; several, such as Halle's and Higbee's, were still renovating and updating their downtown stores in the 1960s. The writing was on the wall, however, as Euclid Avenue started to lose some of its luster, Cleveland's population growth slowed and shifted outward, and the retail industry consolidated at an increasing pace.

Those stores that embraced the trend of suburbanization seemed to be the most successful. Sterling-Lindner, which had opted against suburbanization in the 1950s and 1960s, quickly found itself unable to be profitable with just a downtown store and had closed by 1968.

Bailey's, however, showed that even being a pioneer of suburbanization was not a guarantee of success in this new age. Trying an alternate tactic from Sterling-Lindner, by 1963 its store at Ontario and Prospect Avenues had been closed and demolished, with the chain existing only in the suburbs. After being split several times and converted to a discount format, it ultimately was unsuccessful, and by 1968, it too was closed.

Halle's and Higbee's eventually were swept into the nationalization of the department store industry, with Halle's being acquired by Marshall Field's of Chicago and later closed by a retail liquidator. Higbee's remained under local control until being bought out in 1984, and, in the end, landing in the hands of Dillard's stores, which still operate many of the former Higbee's stores in 2009. It also was the last of the downtown stores to fall, remaining open (as Dillard's) until 2002.

The May Company, already a division of the national May's organization, became Kaufmann's in 1993, the same year its downtown store was closed. After several corporate rearrangements, many of its former stores now bear the name of Macy's.

Although many of the local figures are gone, the legacy of Cleveland's department stores still lives on through the buildings and the memories they created.

These ladies and gentlemen are dressed in their best to shop at Higbee's in July 1964.

Halle's storefront featured a plaid sidewalk covering in 1965. Fans of the sitcom *The Drew Carey Show*, set in Cleveland, may recognize the Halle's building as the facade used in the introduction of the show to represent Drew's fictional employer, the Winfred-Louder Department Store.

In a detour from the standard department store fare, Higbee's offered the Shop of Old Things. Opened in 1965 as part of the fifth-floor renovation, the Shop of Old Things featured a selection of gifts and original antiques.

As part of its fifth-floor renovation, Higbee's updated and expanded its book department. The 1960s was a gray area in attitudes about downtown retail; in the 1950s, it was still believed that the suburbs would never surpass the downtown stores in shopping, whereas by the 1970s, the tide of public opinion had largely shifted against the great city stores.

This is a view of the "light and airy" level-three fashion floor at Higbee's from the fur salon.

A view of the May Company's sales floor is seen from up high in 1965.

The men's department at Halle's received a half-million-dollar renovation in 1966. By this time it had become apparent that suburban stores were eating away ever-increasing chunks of business from their downtown counterparts; however, management of area stores continued to attempt to draw shoppers downtown.

A late-1960s addition to Halle's was the Happy Accent shop. Promotional materials described it as a "compendium of collected fun objects such as bentwood chairs, furry pillows, trunks and other adult play things like a political chess set."

Congressman Jim Stanton is seen on Public Square in the midst of a protest of the sale of Farah Pants at the May Company. In 1973, protests were staged by the Amalgamated Clothing Workers of America union in 60 cities across the United States in response to Farah's resistance of unionization at its Texas factory. In order to pressure Farah where it hurt—in the pocketbook—the union called for a boycott and picketed department stores, such as the May Company, where the pants were sold. The boycott resulted in a large drop in sales for Farah, and by 1974, the factory was unionized.

Not only did the 1970s introduce a fabulous array of fashion, it also ushered in the era of the home video game consoles. Not to be left out of this profitable new trend, Higbee's added the systems to its lineup of other electronics such as radios, stereos, televisions, and the like. The salesman above is demonstrating the Fairchild Channel F, a lesser-known game system from that time period.

John Zwek diligently examines the mannequins exhibited in the Higbee's display window in 1977. Although inanimate mannequins were the standard for displaying clothing, occasionally the department stores would hire "living mannequins," live models, to show off the season's latest styles.

In 1979, Halle's featured a large Edwin Mieczkowski mural on the side of its flagship store. Mieczkowski, known for his colorful geometric works of art, taught at the Cleveland Institute of Art for 39 years and has works displayed in museums from Cleveland to Poland.

While Taylor's made inroads into the suburbs, by 1961 the May Company management found operating two competing department stores to be redundant and closed Taylor's just prior to Christmas of that year, with the downtown store being shuttered and the Southgate store being converted to the May's nameplate.

While Bailey's lived on in its suburban stores, by 1963, the flagship store at Prospect and Ontario Avenues had been shuttered. In 1958, longtime corporate parent National Department Stores Company sold Bailey's to Century Food Market Company, which quickly started making changes in order to strengthen the organization. One of the most visible changes was the closure of the downtown flagship store. The May Company, seeking to accommodate the increasing number of shoppers coming downtown via automobile, purchased the neighboring building and quickly demolished it. From the rubble rose a monument to the autocentric shopper of the 1960s: a gleaming new multilevel parking garage with direct access to the May Company building.

From left to right, Cleveland mayor Ralph Locher, city councilman Wilson Latkovic, and May Company general manager Francis A. Coy wield sledgehammers for the first crack at taking down the Bailey Company building in 1963.

Bailey's had been an early adopter of the trend of taking stores to the suburbs, but by the 1960s, even its suburban stores were struggling. In addition to closing down the main store on Ontario Avenue, the East 101st Street store, in a neighborhood that had ceased being "outlying" long before, was closed. Continuing to try to right itself, in 1965, the Lakewood store was sold to competing chain Neville's. Neville's had no more success than Bailey's, and the store was closed in 1968.

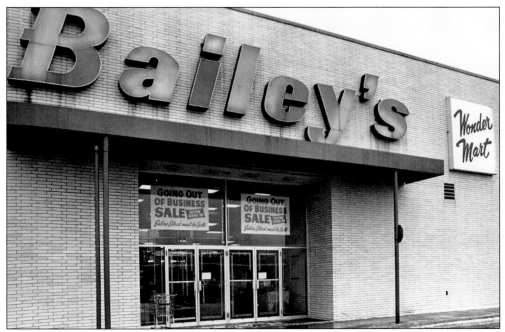

One of the last remaining Bailey's stores, at Eastgate Plaza in Mayfield Heights, appears during its closing sale in 1967. By this time, the three remaining Bailey's stores were a branch of Wonder Mart, Inc., which was a subsidiary of owner Century Food Markets Company and had been converted to a discount retailer format. Even with the change in strategy, Bailey's was not successful, and the last stores were closed.

When suburbanization of the retail trade hit its stride in the late 1950s and early 1960s, Sterling-Lindner ignored it. Management felt that the store was in an excellent location across from Halle's in Playhouse Square and that building outlying branches would simply detract from the main store. Unfortunately for Sterling-Lindner, the 1960s decline of downtown shopping led to a harsh reality. By the time Sterling management realized the error in not expanding, it was too late, and the store closed its doors for the last time in September 1968.

Remaining merchandise in the jewelry department is boxed up during the closure of the downtown Halle's store in 1982. In November 1981, the Halle's chain, then owned by Chicago retailer Marshall Field, was sold to Columbus-based Associated Investor's Corporation, owner of the Value City chain. Although initially the company indicated it would continue operating Halle's into the future, it did an about-face in early 1982, abruptly closing all the stores.

Several customers peruse the linen section of Halle's during its closeout sale in 1982. By this time, the last vestige of the Halle family had been gone from the company for nearly a decade.

Although the surprise 1982 closing of the Halle's chain was a blow to Cleveland, it was a boon to area bargain shoppers. Halle's stores throughout the region held massive clearance sales, and the downtown store was no exception. At right, a shopper struggles with an armful of lamps and shopping bags purchased at the sale.

Higbee's was the next to leave local control, being sold in 1984 to Industrial Equity Limited, followed by another sale in 1988 to a partnership between Dillard's and local mall magnate Edward J. Debartolo. Debartolo intended to combine Higbee's with Pittsburgh-based Horne's under a plan that did not come to fruition. Debartolo is shown above (left) with Horne's president Vincent Fanoli (right) discussing plans for Randall Park Mall in 1973.

125

Although a part of the national May Company chain, May Company of Cleveland management still had significant local control. In 1989, May's of Cleveland was combined with Akron-based (and May's-owned) O'Neil's to form May Company of Ohio. By 1993, May Company of Ohio was merged with May property Kaufmann's of Pittsburgh, erasing the May's name in Ohio and removing local control. At the same time, the declining Public Square store was closed. Pictured is the former May's of Ohio store at Rolling Acres Mall in Akron. (Rollingacres.org.)

In 2005, the national May's organization was purchased by Federated Department Stores of Cincinnati, owner of Macy's. By 2006, Kaufmann's stores were rebranded Macy's, as seen above with the former May Company store at Canton Centre Mall in Canton. (Rollingacres.org.)